LIFESKILLS IN ACTION

MONEY SKILLS

P9-CAL-618

Managing Credit

JILL
HANEY

LIFESKILLS IN ACTION
MONEY SKILLS

MONEY

Living on a Budget | Road Trip
Opening a Bank Account | The Guitar
Managing Credit | High Cost
Using Coupons | Get the Deal
Planning to Save | Something Big

LIVING

Smart Grocery Shopping | Shop Smart
Doing Household Chores | Keep It Clean
Finding a Place to Live | A Place of Our Own
Moving In | Pack Up
Cooking Your Own Meals | Dinner Is Served

JOB

Preparing a Resume | Not Her Job
Finding a Job | Dream Jobs
Job Interview Basics | Job Ready
How to Act Right on the Job | Choices
Employee Rights | Not So Sweet

SADDLEBACK
EDUCATIONAL PUBLISHING
www.sdlback.com

ISBN-13: 978-1-68021-012-5
ISBN-10: 1-68021-012-2
eBook: 978-1-63078-296-2

Printed in Malaysia

21 20 19 18 17   3 4 5 6 7

A new pair of shoes.

Tickets to a game.

Food at a grocery store.

These all cost money.

There are many ways to pay.

Some people use cash. Some write checks.

Others pay with a debit card.

It takes money from their bank account.

But many use another kind of card.

A **credit card**.

What is a credit card?

It looks like a debit card.

But it does not work the same way.

A credit card may be from a store.

It may be from a bank.

People use it to pay for things.

This is called **making charges**.

But the money does not come from their bank.

The credit card company pays the store.

It is a loan. People are borrowing the money.

They will get a bill later.

They must pay the credit card company back.

It seems easy.

You can get things **now**.

You pay **later**.

This can really help you out.

You might need something.

Like food. Or gas.

But you are out of cash.

You have a job. Payday is next week.

But you need the food or gas now.

So you use a credit card.

You borrow the money.

This lets you get what you need now.

Then you can pay the bill later.

You will have money then.

A credit card can help in other ways too.

Cash is hard to keep track of.

It is easy to forget where you spend it.

But credit cards make tracking easy.

You make charges.

The credit card company tracks them.

You get your bill.

It lists all your charges.

You can see where you spent your money.

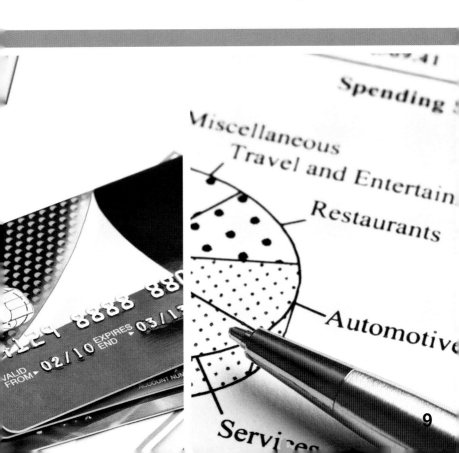

It all sounds good.

But wait. There is more to think about.

Using a credit card means something.

You make a promise.

A **promise** to pay later.

You will need money to pay the bill.

Not paying will get you in big trouble.

It will cost you a lot.

Banks like to give people credit cards.
So do some stores.

They make it easy. They send offers
in the mail.

Why? The cards make them money.

How? They charge **fees**.
They charge **interest**.

That is money you pay.

You need to know how much.

you the benefit of lower ch

and charges,
king, sa

All credit cards charge fees.

A fee is money you have to pay.

Read the letter that comes with the card.

The words will be small.

But they are there.

Look for fees.

See how much they are.

They could be $20, $35, or more.

It adds up.

Some credit cards have **annual fees**.

You pay every year.

You must pay if you want to use the card.

Not every card has this fee.

Look for ones that don't.

Credit cards have rules.

There are fees if you break the rules.

Your bill will have a due date.

What if you pay late?

There will be a fee. A **late fee**.

You will owe more money.

Credit cards have **limits**.

The limit is how much you can spend.

It might be $1,000. Or $2,500.

What if you spend more than that?

There will be a fee.

You pay more money.

credit card statement
Posting Date
Rate Code
Description of Transactions
Balance from previous page
PAYMENT PROTECTION COVER
ON BALANCE OF 4,735.07
INTEREST CHARGED
EST INTEREST-NEXT STATEMENT
Available to spend

VALID FROM
ORDER PAYMENT
PAYMENT FEE CHARGED
INTEREST

Fees cost you. So does interest.

Look at the letter that comes with your card.

It will show an APR.

That stands for **annual percentage rate**.

Every credit card has one.

It may be 10%. It may be 20%.

That is how much interest you will pay.

How does it work?

You use a credit card. You spend $500.

The bill comes. You owe $500. But you only pay $50.

That means you are borrowing money longer.

The next month you don't owe $450. You owe more.

Interest has been added.

APR is important.

The more it is, the more you pay.

Look for cards with low APR.

Do you want a credit card?

Many people do.

A card can be a big help.

And it might not cost you anything.

How? It's all about being smart.

Choose a good card. Be smart about how you use it.

Make the credit card **work for you**.

First, pick the right card.

Shop around. There are many good deals.

Find a card with no annual fee.

Look for a low APR.

Some cards have **rewards**.

You may be able to get cash back.

Or points to get things.

Like gift cards.

Or trips.

Check out each deal. But don't be fooled.

Rewards are nice.

But no fees and low APR are better.

Promotional

0%

APR

for a limited

time

Did you find a card you liked? One that was right for you?

You won't have to wait long. Your new card will come in the mail.

Be smart. Think of it like cash.

Keep it in a safe place. Don't let friends use it.

Cards can be stolen. So can card numbers.

Know where your card is at all times.

If it does get lost, report it.

Call the card company.

Do this right away.

Ready to make a charge? Look at the cost.

Know how much money you have to spend.

Don't charge more than that.

That way you can **pay the card off**.

A bill will come each month.

It will show your **balance**. That is everything you owe.

It will also show a payment amount.

You must pay at least this much.

But it won't be all you owe.

It will only be a part.

Pay more than that. Pay all if you can.

If you pay it all, you won't pay interest.

Pay it on time too. Then you won't pay fees.

That is the smart way to use a credit card.

What if you do charge too much?

The bill comes. You don't have enough money.

You can't pay it off.

This happens. It is easy to do with a credit card.

But be smart about it.

Put the card away. Cut it up if you have to.

Then pay what you can. It may take a few months.

You will pay interest each month.

But keep paying on time.

Work to pay it off. You will be glad you did.

Being smart will help you.

You may want to buy a car someday.

You may need a loan.

Banks will look at your **credit score**.

The score must be good to get a loan.

How can you get a good score?

Credit Score	Description
760 – 849	Excellent
700 – 759	Great
	Good

Have a credit card. Charge small things on it.

Pay all you owe each month.

Pay it on time.

This shows you are a good borrower.

Your score will go up.

It will be easier to get a loan.

A credit card is useful.

You don't have to carry cash.

You can track your charges.

It can help your credit score.

But it makes it easy to spend.

You can charge too much.

So you have to be smart.

Keep track. Only spend what you can afford.

Pay off the card each month.

Make the card work for you.

HIGH
COST

PJ Gray

LIFESKILLS IN ACTION

MONEY SKILLS

MONEY

Living on a Budget | Road Trip
Opening a Bank Account | The Guitar
Managing Credit | High Cost
Using Coupons | Get the Deal
Planning to Save | Something Big

LIVING

Smart Grocery Shopping | Shop Smart
Doing Household Chores | Keep It Clean
Finding a Place to Live | A Place of Our Own
Moving In | Pack Up
Cooking Your Own Meals | Dinner Is Served

JOB

Preparing a Resume | Not Her Job
Finding a Job | Dream Jobs
Job Interview Basics | Job Ready
How to Act Right on the Job | Choices
Employee Rights | Not So Sweet

SADDLEBACK
EDUCATIONAL PUBLISHING
www.sdlback.com

ISBN-13: 978-1-68021-012-5
ISBN-10: 1-68021-012-2
eBook: 978-1-63078-296-2

Printed in Malaysia

21 20 19 18 17   3 4 5 6 7

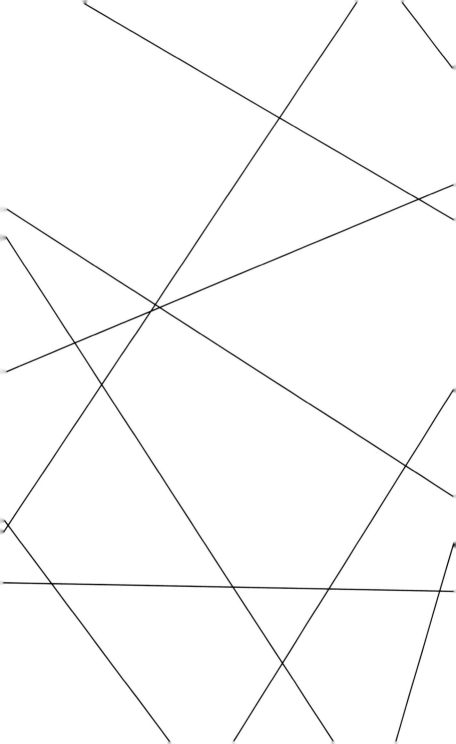

"You have mail," said Kim's mom.

Kim was sitting at the kitchen table. She had to go to work soon.

Kim was looking at her cell phone. There were a lot of photos from last night. The party was fun. She looked good in her cap and gown.

High school was over for Kim. She still lived with her mom. But she hoped to move out soon. She wanted her own place.

Kim's mom sat down. "Did you see your mail?" she asked.

Kim opened her mail. It was her new credit card.

"A credit card?" Kim's mom asked. "Is that a good idea?"

Kim rolled her eyes. "Why not?" Kim asked. "Don't you trust me?"

"It's not that," her mom said.

Kim rolled her eyes. "Sure," she said. "If you say so."

Kim got up. She grabbed her purse and car keys. "I have to go to work."

Her mom grabbed her arm. "Wait," her mom said. "Let's talk about this."

"Why?" Kim asked. "I'm not a kid."

"I know that," her mom replied.

Kim was mad. Her mom should trust her. She was an adult now.

She had a job. She had worked at the jeans store for two years. She paid for her cell phone bill. She bought some of her own clothes. She drove her mom's old car. She bought her own gas.

"Please sit down," her mom asked. "Just for a second."

Kim sat down again. Her mom looked at her. "Why do you want a card?"

Kim did not speak at first. She was thinking.

Her mind took her back. Back to when she decided to get a credit card. It was a month ago.

She was at the mall with Alison. Alison was her best friend. They worked at the jeans store together. Alison and Kim had the day off. They were looking at clothes.

"I like your new purse," Kim said.

Alison smiled. "Thanks. I got it online."

Kim wanted to shop online. She had a debit card from her bank. But she did not have enough money in her account.

"You should check out their site," Alison said. "They have more than just purses. They have a lot of cute shoes. And they have great sales."

Kim nodded and smiled. Alison pulled out her new cell phone. She tapped the phone with her finger. She gave the phone to Kim.

"Look," Alison said. "This is the site."

Kim nodded at the phone.

"Those are the shoes," Alison said. "The ones I told you about. I bought those last night. They should get here next week."

Alison was holding a pile of clothes.
"Are you buying all of those?" Kim asked.

"Sure!" Alison replied. "I'll just put them on my card."

Kim watched Alison buy the clothes.
She was happy for her friend. But she felt a little jealous.

"Are you going to the concert next week?" Alison asked. "We are all going. We are getting hotel rooms too. And we'll stop at the outlet mall. It is on the way. I can't wait."

Kim wantcd to go. But the trip would cost a lot of money. "I don't think I can afford it," Kim said.

"Why not? Just use your credit card."

Kim said nothing.

"Don't you have one?" Alison asked.

Kim shook her head. Alison felt bad for saying it. They said nothing as they left the store.

Alison smiled at Kim. "I can lend you money for the trip."

"No thanks," Kim said.

"But I really want you to go!"

"Me too," Kim said. "But I can't."

Kim looked at Alison's shopping bags. They kept walking.

"Let's grab a bite to eat," Alison said. "My treat."

"Are you sure?" Kim asked.

"Sure." Alison smiled.

They ate at the burger place. Alison paid for their food with her credit card.

"Let's go to one more store," Alison said.

"Sure," said Kim.

They walked past a shoe store. "Wow!" Alison said at the store window. "Look at that pair!"

"Those are hot," Kim said. "But look at the price."

"I want them," Alison said. "I want to wear those to the concert. They would look so hot with my jeans."

Alison went into the store. She asked for the shoes in her size. They fit perfectly. So Alison bought them. She paid with her credit card.

Alison and Kim left the mall. Alison drove Kim home in her new car.

"How do you like the car?" Kim asked.

"It's great. I love it!"

Kim smiled. "Did you buy it with a credit card?" she joked.

"Yes, I did," Alison replied.

"What?" Kim asked. "You are kidding!"

"No joke," Alison said. "I did buy it with my credit card. And the card company gave me a gift."

"A gift?"

"A plane ticket!" Alison said.

"No way!" Kim replied. "Why?"

"I spent so much money using the card."

"Kim!" Kim's mom said. "Did you hear me?"

"What?" Kim asked. She had gotten lost in her thoughts.

"Why do you want a credit card?" her mom asked. "Do you need money?"

Kim waited. She looked down at her feet.

"I want a new car," Kim said. "I can use the card to get it."

"Please don't do that."

"Why not?" Kim asked. "I can use the card. I can get a new car now. I won't have to wait."

The credit card had come with a letter. Kim's mom picked it up. She pushed the letter to Kim. "Did you read the fine print?"

"What fine print?" Kim asked.

"You made a deal with this card company."

Kim picked up the letter. She acted like she read it. "Don't worry, Mom," Kim said. "I will pay every month. And I will pay on time."

"I'm sure you will," she said. "But there's more to it."

Kim's mom put her finger on the paper. "See this fee?" she asked. "You must pay a fee. You have to pay it every year. Just to use the card."

Kim's mom moved her finger on the paper. "See this number?" she asked. "It is the rate. The rate of interest charged each month. Think of the card as a loan. They loaned you money. Now they will charge you interest. Interest is money added to what you owe. That means you pay more money each month."

"So?" Kim said. "I will pay every month. I will keep up with my bill."

"Yes, but they only make you pay some each month. You pay interest on the rest. It will take years to pay it off. In the end, you will pay twice as much. The car will cost you double the price."

"But I need to build credit," Kim said. "A credit card helps you do that. You told me so."

"Yes," said her mom. "But you can build credit safely. You can use your card for small things."

"Like clothes?" Kim asked.

"Yes," her mom said. "Just don't overdo it. Pay every month on time. Pay all you owe. Then you will not pay extra. And you will build good credit."

"What will good credit get me?" Kim asked.

"It proves that you are good with your money. Banks will trust you more. You can get a loan. A loan with a low interest rate."

"Like a loan for a new car?"

"Yes," her mom said. "Or for a home of your own."

Kim smiled at her mom. "I get it, Mom. Thanks."

Her mom smiled back. "I have one more thing," her mom said. Kim's mom pulled a paper from her purse.

"What is this?" Kim asked.

"It's my credit card bill."

Kim looked at the bill. Her mom owed a lot.

"Our trip to the lake last year?" her mom asked. "Your birthday party? My new car tires?"

"Yes," Kim said. "What about them?"

"I used a credit card."

"Oh, Mom."

Kim stopped to think. "Wait! Your new night job," Kim said.

"Yes," her mom said. "I had to get a second job. I spent too much. Now I need to pay this bill off. As fast as I can."

"Oh, Mom. I didn't know."

"You see," her mom said. "A credit card can help you. Or it can hurt you. It's up to you."

Kim hugged her mom. "Thanks for telling me, Mom. And thanks for your help."

Her mom smiled. Then she looked at her watch. "We need to hurry. Or we will both be late for work!"

JUST *flip* THE BOOK!

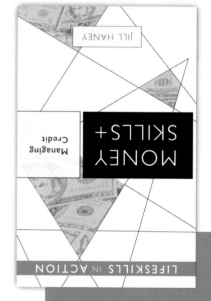

JILL HANEY

MONEY SKILLS+

Managing Credit

LIFESKILLS IN ACTION

Do you think Kim will make the right choice when it comes to her new credit card? Want to find out more about credit cards and how to manage them!

What happens when a person is not smart with a credit card? That is what Kim is about to find out in *High Cost*. Want to read on?

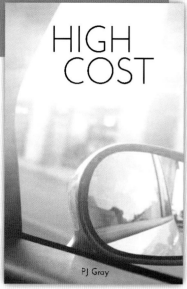

HIGH COST

PJ Gray

JUST *flip* THE BOOK!